For Mat and Ben – SS

This edition published 2007
By Zero To Ten Limited
Part of the Evans Publishing Group
2A Portman Mansions, Chiltern Street, London W1U 6NR

Text copyright © Evans Brothers Limited 2005
Illustrations copyright © Tim Archbold 2005

British Library Cataloguing in Publication Data
Swallow, Su
        A head full of stories.
        1. Children's stories - Pictorial works
        I. Title
        823.9'14 [J]

ISBN 1 84089 484 9
13 digit ISBN 978 1 84089 484 4

A Head Full of Stories

by Su Swallow

illustrated by Tim Archbold

ZERO TO TEN

"Jack!"

"Story time!"

"No!" shouted Jack.
"My head is full up with stories."

"You tell me
a story, then."

So Jack told Mum about Cinderella.

He told Dad a story too.

And Grandma…

and Grandad...

and his brother…

and the cat...

and Teddy.

"My head's empty now!"

"Tell me a story please!"

"Oh!"